not a guide to

Torbay

Anthony Poulton-Smith

The
History
Press

First published in 2012

The History Press
The Mill, Brimscombe Port
Stroud, Gloucestershire, GL5 2QG
www.thehistorypress.co.uk

British Library Cataloguing in Publication Data.
A catalogue record for this book is available from the British Library.

ISBN 978 0 7524 6882 2

Typesetting and origination by The History Press
Printed in Great Britain

SALUS ❖ ET ❖ FELICITAS

Little more than a coded map of the area, the colours depict Torbay's blue sea, gold sandy beaches and red Devon soil.

*

The flag of St George with streamers
shows links to the Royal Navy.

*

The letter T is for Torbay.

*

Note the four crenellations of the crown, one for each of the four councils which united to form Torbay. Elements of various Arms unite to produce the above image: Devon County Council, William of Orange, the Ferrers family, Torquay, Paignton and Brixham.

*

Beneath is the motto *Salubritas et Felicitas*,
the Latin for 'Health and Happiness'.

Contents

What's in a Name?

The modern name adds the 'bay' to the tor or 'rocky outcrop' which also gave a name to Torquay ('the quayside by the rocky outcrop').

Paignton describes itself as 'the farmstead associated with a man called Paega', a Saxon name, followed by '*ing tun*' ('farmstead associated with'). Brixham is 'the homestead of a man called Brioc', a Celtic name, added to the Old English *ham* ('homestead'). Babbacombe describes 'the *cumb* or valley of a man called Babba'.

Paignton Pier

In 1874 the Paignton Pier Act received the official go-ahead. Work took eight months, with George Soudon Bridgeman's design opening in June 1879. The original pier was 780ft long, 40ft more than today's. By 1881 the pier-head was enlarged to include a billiard room, not something we would expect to find today.

These buildings were destroyed by a fire in 1919 and, although some repairs were undertaken, went into a slow decline. In 1940, following the outbreak of war, the pier was one of the many severed as a defensive measure and repaired after the war. It was not until the 1980s that the neck of the pier was widened and rebuilt, with further restoration work in the 1990s making it appear much as it does today.

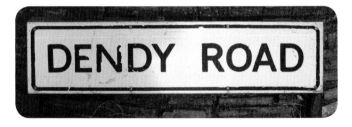

The Mallock Memorial Tower, Torquay

Completed in 1902, ownership of the memorial was passed to the local council in an official ceremony on 7 March 1903. This piece of Bath stone, designed by Bournemouth architect John Donkin and sculpted by Harry Herris of Exeter, now acts as a traffic island at the junction of the Strand, Torwood Street and Victoria Parade.

Being erected in the middle of a busy junction has effectively isolated this impressive memorial. Not only has this made its origins a mystery to most but it has also made it difficult to maintain. Over the last century the salt and traffic pollution have certainly taken their toll. Funded by subscription, it honours Richard Mallock.

Member of Parliament for Torquay between 1886 and 1895, Mallock also served the town as a magistrate for many years. His family purchased the manor of Cockington from the Carys for the princely sum of £10,000 in 1654, and were resident at Cockington Court until the twentieth century. Richard Mallock was particularly popular, a major philanthropist who spent much time and money on maintaining and promoting Cockington and Torquay.

Many have wondered why Torquay's railway station is so far from the town itself. When Brunel brought the line to Torbay, the owners of Torre Abbey refused to allow their lands to be crossed. It was Richard Mallock who stepped forward and permitted the railway to be built on his land. Hence Torquay Station should correctly be known as Cockington Station, for it is officially a part of Cockington.

Napoleonic Fort, Berry Head

Always a desirable location, Berry Head was certainly occupied in the Iron Age, when a great rampart of 18ft in height surrounded the settlement. Evidence of Roman occupation has also been found, but what we see today are the remains of the early nineteenth-century defences.

There was an earlier battery here, housing some 800 or 900 men. However, the conditions were reported as being far from ideal: sanitation was poor, huts in poor repair, no mess, no kitchens, no medical facilities. What we see today is a result of an Act of Parliament in 1794. Two years of work ended in 1805, during which time the Iron Age ramparts were destroyed in order to produce two forts and three temporary batteries. A thousand men were stationed here, some from the Royal Artillery and others from the Dorset Militia (the latter commanded by the same man who produced the damning report in 1798, one Colonel J.P. Bastard). The castle or round top battery is the oldest of the fortifications, most likely originating in the reign of Henry VIII.

These Napoleonic defences were permanently occupied until, by 1830, a single individual acted as caretaker. He passed his days doing a little maintenance, accompanied by the wild birds and the domesticated sheep, and watching the quarrymen eating away at the base of the rock. He must have been here some time, for it is noted he was cultivating his own cabbages and potatoes among the ruins.

Beach Huts

A quintessential element of the traditional British resort, the beach hut is equally loved and loathed. The idea began with the bathing machines of the Victorian era. The beach hut provided a permanent place to change, shelter from wind or rain and later a clean water supply and possibly electrical power. Thus, occupants could make a cup of tea, store deckchairs, bathing clothes and towels.

Purpose-built huts were constructed to add to those adapted from former fisherman's huts and were popular until all beaches were closed during the Second World War. By the 1950s, the heyday of British resorts, beach huts were in great demand. Brightly coloured, there are examples around the coastline of Torbay, the majority found at Preston Sands, Goodrington and Broadsands, although there are still some left in Torquay. They are as much a part of imagery associated with British beaches as the pier, Punch and Judy show and donkey rides.

In recent years there has been a revival of interest in the beach hut, resulting in escalating prices. In 2009 the Telegraph reported newly-built huts fetching prices as low as £15,000 and as high as £150,000, while one restored vintage chalet sold for an astonishing £290,000. No such money exchanges hands in Torbay, where all the beach huts are owned by the local council and can be hired for £63 per week in peak periods, with the option to join fellow users in the club known as the Mad Hutters.

Torquay Views

Taking advantage of Torbay's subtropical climate, a network of paths meandered up the cliff between borders planted with such flora as bamboo, yuccas and similar species.

In 1920, the film industry utilised this area as a location for jungle settings, and Cairn's Torquay Film Co. produced their version of Warwick Deeping's *Unrest* here. Originally known as the Fisherman's Walk, the installation of soft lighting coincided with a change of name to the Royal Terrace Gardens.

In March 2007, an inspection revealed that many of the trees and shrubs had severely weakened the rock face. Early the following year, crowds watched from a safe distance as trees, shrubs and overgrown scrub were removed. A load in excess of 300 tonnes of vegetation was taken away. During and after the operation, further rock falls resulted in unsightly, but necessary, temporary boarding being erected.

Unfortunately, 'temporary' turned into several years, until the spring of 2011, in fact, when the cliff was finally made safe, some seating provided and new lighting installed. However, the major difference was the floating path with handrail ('floating' as it is not cut into the face as previously but supported away from the face proper). This now leads to a viewing platform offering superb views over Torquay and the bay beyond.

The Torquay Land Train

In 1994 Chris Griffin bought a land train from Weymouth. For twelve years this white train was a familiar sight snaking up and down the promenade at Paignton until it was shipped off to Holyhead and the operator headed off to Torquay.

The red land train is fifteen years old, Chris bought it five years ago. Made at Chandler's Ford, it has a turbo-charged, six cylinder engine and with more breaks than a jumbo jet! Running a route which takes in the pedestrianised shopping centre, down to the Strand near the harbour and along the front as far as Torquay Station, this vehicle works for at least ten months of the year, carrying upwards of 70,000 passengers.

Chris admits to approaching pensionable age but, in his words, 'I'm too old to retire!' Talking about future plans, he revealed a desire for a new vehicle, one based on the famous trams of San Francisco (though there are several logistical problems to overcome before that becomes a reality).

Torbay Place Names

Torbay: 'The bay of the place called Torre'. The name was first used in the late sixteenth century.

Torquay: 'The landing place near the rocky place'. Not recorded before 1591.

Paignton: 'Paega's farmstead'. A name first seen in the Domesday Book.

Brixham: 'The homestead of a man called Brioc'. The earliest record is again in the Domesday Book.

Babbacombe: 'The valley of a man called Babba'. First seen in around 1200.

St Marychurch: 'The church of St Mary'. A name first recorded in around 1050.

Preston: 'The farmstead of the priests'. No surviving record from before 1830.

Churston: 'The farmstead associated with a church'. It is in the Domesday Book.

Broadsands: Exactly what it says! A comparatively modern name.

Blagdon: 'The dark hill'. Appears as 'Blakedone' in 1242.

Cockington: 'The farmstead of a man called Cocca'. First noted in the Domesday record.

Watcombe: 'The valley where wheat is grown'. Recorded as Whatecomb in 1414.

Berry Head: 'The fortified place'.

Chelston: 'The farmstead of a man called Ceola'.

Corbyn Head: 'The carved nose'. Purported to be how this headland looked.

Daddyhole: 'Demon or devil's hole'.

FISHER STREET

KNICK KNACK LANE

Galmpton: 'The farmstead of the fee-paying folk' (i.e. it was rented).

Gerston: 'The grassy farmstead'.

Goodrington: 'The farmstead associated with a man called Godhere'.

Hollicombe: 'The sunken valley'.

Hopes Nose: 'The headland by the blind valley'.

Livermead: 'The rushy meadow'.

Oddicombe: 'The point of the valley'.

Roundham: 'The rough homestead'.

Shiphay: 'The enclosure for sheep'.

And of course, everywhere has some quirky street names. Torbay has:

Blackball Lane

Blindwylle Road

Dashpers

Dosson Grove

Garlic Rea

Gramercy Fields

Ipplepen Road

Jacolind Walk

Knick Knack Lane

Stabb Close

The Greebys

The Gurneys

The Saddle

Weekaborough Drive

Distance From…

Place	Miles	Kilometres
London	166	267
Dublin, Republic of Ireland	231	371
Paris, France	286	461
Belfast, Northern Ireland	303	488
Edinburgh	380	612
Frankfurt, Germany	540	869
Vatican City	966	1,554
Reykjavik, Iceland	1,158	1,864
Gibraltar	1,295	2,085
Istanbul, Turkey	1,681	2,706
Moscow, Russia	1,720	2,768
Cairo, Egypt	2,279	3,668
Jerusalem, Israel	2,355	3,790
North Pole	2,733	4,398
New York, USA	3,341	5,377
Detroit, USA	3,646	5,867
Centre of the Earth	3,975	6,397
Rio de Janeiro, Brazil	4,875	7,845
Mexico City, Mexico	5,428	8,736
Cape Town, South Africa	5,982	9,627
Tokyo, Japan	6,082	9,788
Hong Kong, China	6,140	9,882
Lima, Peru	6,157	9,909
Hawaii	7,276	11,710
Falkland Islands	7,786	12,530
South Pole	9,706	15,620
Sydney, Australia	10,725	17,260
Wellington, New Zealand	11,800	18,990
The Moon	238,857	384,403

Twinned Towns

Hamelin, Lower Saxony, Germany

A town on the River Weser and the capital of Hamelin-Pyrmont district, Hamelin has a population of around 60,000. Famous for the folk tale of the Pied Piper, this former Prussian town has proved an important location in many European conflicts. Surrounded by four fortresses, it was the best protected town in the former Kingdom of Hanover.

During the Second World War the local prison was used to hold political prisoners by the Nazis. At least 200 people died here when it was under Nazi control, and more when the Allies advanced in 1945. Fittingly, German war criminals were kept here awaiting trial. Around 200 were hanged here after being found guilty. The building is now a hotel.

Hellevoetsluis, Voorne-Putten Island, Netherlands

A small city of some 30,000 inhabitants. Close to the broad landscape of Zeeland, the name Hellevoetsluis means 'the lock at the foot of the Helle', the Helle being a local river, which has disappeared due to erosion and deposition.

Once a canal linked the town to Rotterdam, though when ships grew too large for the Kanaal door Voorne, the town fell into decline. Shipyards closed, and the naval base relocated, while 75 per cent of the town was destroyed by German forces in 1944, who had previously used it as a base for submarines. Since the war the town has seen a sharp upturn in fortune as the ports, which took trade away from Hellevoetsluis, Europoort and Rotterdam, required housing for the huge workforce and new development here doubled the population within a few short years. Links between Hellevoetsluis and Torbay date back to 1688, when the fleet of William of Orange embarked *en route* for Brixham with his 'invasion fleet'.

Historical Timeline

Torre Abbey founded by monks. Evidence of monks fishing in Torbay.

The Spanish Armada vessel *Senora del Rosario* is captured in the bay, and prisoners are held in the Tithe Barn of Torre Abbey.

Earliest specific record of Christian worship in Torbay in St Marychurch.

John Cary purchases Cockington Manor.

Cary family sell Cockington to the Mallock family.

Consecration of the chapel at Torre Abbey.

c.925　1196　1373　1588　1654　1779

1070　1260　1539　1595　1688

Osbern, Bishop of Exeter, built wall and tower at Paignton.

Henry VIII closes Torre Abbey as part of the Dissolution of the Monasteries.

Prince of Orange and future King William III lands at Brixham *en route* to London.

Parish church built at Paignton, the third on the site; it was rebuilt in the nineteenth century.

Sir George Cary expands the family lands with the purchase of St Marychurch.

Bath House, later the Regina Hotel, opened, offering warm and cold sea-water bathing.

Construction of Brixham breakwater begins. It was completed in 1916.

Singer family trustees oversee construction of the sea wall at Preston.

Princess Victoria pays her first visit to Torquay, arriving at the quay on *Emerald*.

Torbay hit by a hurricane, with the loss more than thirty vessels and at least 100 lives.

1817   **1833**   **1843**   **1866**   **1876**

1793   **1825**   **1838**   **1848**   **1873**

John McEnery of Torre Abbey begins sixteen-year exploration of Kent's Cavern.

First train arrives at Torquay Station (now Torre Station).

'ar declared on France; ritish fleet present in orbay until 1815.

Official approval in Parliament for building of Paignton Harbour.

Construction of Oldway Mansion begins.

Beacon Quay power station brings the first electricity to Torbay.

King George V visits Torbay to review the British fleet.

Winter Gardens begin at Torquay; they were sold to Great Yarmouth twenty-two years later for £1,300.

Bus service begins between Paignton and Torquay.

Torquay tramway extended Paignton.

1881　　**1898**　　**1904**　　**1910**　　**1911**

1879　　**1881**　　**1904**　　**1907**　　**1910**

Paignton Pier opens and layout of Paignton Green beings.

Berry Head Lighthouse is lit for the first time.

First road signs seen in Paigton.

Paignton Club opens. It is still in use, opposite the end of Sands Road.

Tramway opens in Torquay and in five days exceeds 20,000 passengers.

German U-boat
attacks Brixham's
trawler fleet.

*Torbay Herald
and Express*
first published.

Paignton
Pier burns
as watching
crowds line the
promenade.

Torquay United
AFC play their
first game in the
Football League.

1916　　　**1919**　　**1925**　　　**1927**

1914　　**1918**　　**1923**　　**1926**　　**1928**

Seaplane base in
Torquay Harbour
at beginning of
First World War.

Primley Zoological
Gardens founded
by Herbert Whitley
(now Paignton Zoo).

All Saints'
church,
Brixham, first
chimes the
hymn *Abide
With Me.*

No official celebration of
Armistice as influenza
epidemic is killing more
than the war.

First passengers carried
on the Babbacombe
Cliff Railway.

Cockington's Drum
Inn opens its doors
for the first time.

Many troops
arrive in Torbay
as a prelude to
D-Day landings.

Cliff Gardens
and Promenade
opened at
Roundham Head.

Outbreak of the
Second World War;
coastal battery
built at Brixham.

Torquay's
Princess
Theatre opens.

| 1931 | 1936 | 1939 | 1944 | 1961 |
| 1934 | 1938 | 1940 | 1948 | |

Last tram runs
between Torquay
and Paignton.

Belgian refugees
land at Brixham.

Library in Lymington
Road opens, replacing
the original one built
thirty-one years earlier.

London Olympics:
Torbay is the venue
for yachting events.

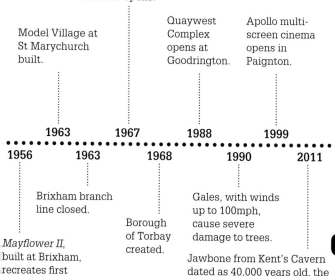

Paigton Festival
Theatre opens.

Model Village at
St Marychurch
built.

Quaywest
Complex
opens at
Goodrington.

Apollo multi-
screen cinema
opens in
Paignton.

1963   1967   1988   1999

1956   1963   1968   1990   2011

Brixham branch
line closed.

Borough
of Torbay
created.

Gales, with winds
up to 100mph,
cause severe
damage to trees.

Mayflower II,
built at Brixham,
recreates first
settler's voyage to
the New World.

Jawbone from Kent's Cavern
dated as 40,000 years old, the
earliest anatomically human
fossil in North-West Europe.

Demography

Torbay has a population of 134,300

Single people (never married): 26,880

Married (including remarried): 53,327

Divorced: 14,273

Widowed: 11,905

Religion:
Christian: 98,820

Buddhist: 196

Hindu: 66

Jewish: 159

Muslim: 341

Sikh: 50

Other: 476

No religion (or none stated): 29,598

More than 26 per cent of the population, significantly higher than the national average of 21 per cent, are over sixty years old – proof the area continues to be a place of retirement. Conversely, of the lower age group only 23 per cent are under the age of twenty, or slightly less than the national average of 25 per cent.

A Summer Day in the Life of the Bay

05:00 – At first light, the fishermen's catch is unloaded and for sale on the dockside at Brixham.

06:00 – The first wreck-fishing trips depart from the harbours at Torquay, Paignton and Brixham.

06:30 – The fire is lit under the boiler of the steam engine of the Paignton and Dartmouth Steam Railway.

07:00 – A tractor descends to the beaches of Preston and Paignton for the daily clean.

09:30 – The pier gates open to the first visitors of the day.

10:00 – The whistle of a steam train announces the departure of the first train from Queen's Park Station *en route* to Dartmouth.

10:30 – Across the bay, ferries depart taking passengers to destinations with no possibility of traffic jams.

12:00 – Horse-drawn traps take visitors to Cockington Manor for the very best of Devon's cream teas.

18:00 – BMAD (Bikers Make A Difference) sees hundreds of motorcycles descend on Paignton Esplanade to raise money for the Air Ambulance, St John's Ambulance, and Torbay Young Carers.

19:30 – Stage curtains at Babbacome, Torquay and Paignton drawn to herald another night of top-class entertainment.

22:00 – A grand fireworks display is a highlight of the regatta.

How Many Times a Year...

5,256,000
Number of double flashes of the lighthouse on Berry Head.

2,000,000
Number of times every year the bay welcomes a visitor.

201,600
The annual number of splashes at Quay West signalling the end of another journey down one of the water park's five slides.

2,196
Number of times the level crossing gates on the Paignton and Dartmouth Steam Railway are closed at Paignton (the same number at Kingswear).

730
Number of high tides (and the same number of low tides).

23
Number of home league fixtures for Torquay United Football Club.

12
Number of meetings of the local council.

Famous for…

… being the setting for one of the most successful British television comedies of all time.

Written by John Cleese and his first wife, Connie Booth, *Fawlty Towers* is based on Cleese's experiences at the Gleneagles Hotel while on location filming *Monty Python's Flying Circus*. Cleese was undoubtedly making notes when the inspiration for Basil, owner Donald Sinclair, threw Eric Idle's briefcase out of the window, believing it to be unsafe!

Note: the series was not filmed here.

I Love...

... Torbay. Every part of the shoreline around the bay has its own identity: Paignton is the perfect place for a beach holiday and ideal for families, be it day or night; Torquay has shops, a marina, and nightlife; and Brixham is slower paced, everyone's idea of a quiet fishing village.

Paignton, Torquay and Brixham are all served by an excellent network of public transport; you can travel easily by land, rail or sea, and thus there is no need to drive the car!

I Hate…

… The balloon. Officially called the 'Torquay Hi Flyer', this balloon was launched in 2009. Tethered near Torre Abbey in Torquay, it lifts a cage carrying paying passengers high into the sky. Reaching a maximum height of 400ft, it takes five minutes to ascend and another five to descend either side of a 'flying time' of fifteen minutes.

This blot on the landscape most often attracts just one word: 'eyesore'!

Films and Television Shoots

Several Monty Python sketches were filmed here. John Cleese rode an open-top bus from Paignton to Torquay while recording his famous 'And now for something completely different' links. Paignton Pier was the backdrop for another series of links, while Scott of the Sahara was filmed on Goodrington's sandy beach.

When the Python team made it to the big screen, they recorded the scene where King Arthur fought and dismembered the Black Knight in Occombe Woods. Despite this long link with the area, *Life of Brian* was not shown here until almost thirty years after the film's release – several authorities gave it an X certification after it was attacked by religious leaders.

As the team refused to allow it to be shown with such a rating, it was never screened around the bay. A special application by the organisers of the bay Comedy Film Festival 2008 uncovered the fact that it was still on the blacklist!

Several other series took advantage of the mild climate to film scenes allegedly shot in more exotic locations. Roger Moore hardly had a hair out of place when he filmed the 1960s series *The Saint* here. Sharp eyes will spot that 'Cannes' in the 1966 episode entitled 'The Better Mousetrap' is actually Torquay Harbour.

Moore returned in the 1970s with co-star Tony Curtis to film *The Persuaders*. The 'Hotel Don Juan', said to be in Spain, is clearly in Torquay.

For seventy-four episodes in the 1970s and 1980s, The Goodies rode high in the list of viewing figures. Their '2001 and a Bit' episode, a poorly disguised spoof of the James Caan film *Rollerball*, was largely filmed in Torquay, the sporting scenes taking place at the Recreation Ground.

The 1970s BBC series *Seaside Special* paid several visits here. A summer Saturday night variety show set under the big top, it brought many names of the time to the area. It is largely regarded as representative of everything bad about television at that time, with Mike Batt's theme tune 'Summertime City' epitomising every comment.

Fish Town was filmed in 2011 at Brixham. This ten-part series looks at the people and businesses of the area. Narrated by Kenneth Cranham and broadcast on Sky Atlantic, the series leans more towards the quirky than the documentary.

Several scenes from the 1995 version of *Sense and Sensibility* starring Emma Thompson and Kate Winslet were filmed here: a wedding at Berry Pomeroy church and several scenes at Compton Castle at Marldon, which doubled as Coombe Magna.

The area became the backdrop for the filming of *Questions of the Heart*, an adaptation of a Rosamunde Pilcher novel.

Kent's Cavern has been used several times by programme makers of *Dr Who*. Almost every time the Doctor was portrayed by a different actor.

The 1981 Oscar-winning film *The French Lieutenant's Woman*, starring Meryl Streep and Jeremy Irons, saw several shoreline scenes filmed around the bay.

Buildings and Architecture

Not all buildings have to be imposing structures in order to leave their mark on the landscape – the **Coffin House** at Brixham being one example. At the bottom of the Temperance Steps, in an area known as Ostend in the seventeenth century (being home to a sizable Flemish community), stands an extraordinarily-shaped building which is highly reminiscent of a coffin. It was built by Dick Rounsell, a man who intended to marry the daughter of Captain John Tuckham. Unfortunately, the officer did not consider Rounsell worthy of his daughter's hand and refused to permit the union, saying he would rather see her in a coffin than married to such a fellow. Hence Coffin House was built by Rounsell. Captain Tuckham was thus outwitted, the pair wed, and the marital home was ready following the wedding.

Kirkham House is today owned by English Heritage. Although once documented as the Priest's House (and as Myrtle Cottage around 1600), there is no evidence to support a religious connection. Indeed, the building is certainly more likely to have been home to a family of some standing, perhaps belonging to landowners or wealthy merchants, featuring the classic three-room plan of the fifteenth century. While the outside fits quite well with the twenty-first century surroundings, the interior is a reminder it would have once have been rendered and lime-washed, and noticeably larger than its neighbours.

The Clink is an early cell (known as a lock-up) near St John's Court on the Littlegate Road. It is well preserved but has not been used as a prison since 1867.

The Torbay Picture House in Torbay Road, near both the mainline and steam railway stations, is the property of the latter. It is believed to be the oldest purpose-built cinema in Europe. Although no longer showing films, the present owners are looking at re-opening the building in the near future.

Should it ever show films again, seat two, row two of the circle, will be in great demand as this was the usual seat of Agatha Christie, the novelist being a regular visitor here. (Indeed, readers will recognise the building from descriptions in several of her novels.)

Museums

Torquay Museum features four floors: local studies, shop and café on the ground floor; the Pengelly Hall and Perigal Room, set aside for lecturers and meetings, on the first; artefacts from nearby Kents Cavern and a display on the evolution of the area on the second; and a room dedicated to Agatha Christie, supplemented by a room looking at the days of exploration and at the Egyptians, is on the third.

Brixham Heritage Museum offers an insight into the port and its history, both through the objects on show and the memories of those who have contributed. The old police station building, outside which the old station lamp still hangs, also houses an excellent exhibition of the maritime history of Brixham.

Brixham also has the *Golden Hind*, a replica of Drake's ship, which was the first ever to circumnavigate the globe. There is no better way of showing the cramped conditions aboard the ship, spread over five decks, where sixty men lived, worked and slept during a three-year voyage.

Brixham Battery is the newest museum in Torbay. It is one of just 7 surviving gun batteries built around the British coastline out of an original 116, this being the most complete. Recently, funding has brought the site back to life, with events and tours at various times throughout the year.

Paignton has a doll and toy museum in Winner Street in the old town. It is a private collection featuring exhibits that will be recognised by every generation.

At Goodrington, discover the Seashore Centre, an exhibition of the life found along the shore of the bay and beyond. Perfect for children, who have the opportunity to join a party exploring the shore, which is led by a highly knowledgeable and entertaining guide.

Babbacombe features Bygones. Walk through the building where a street of Victorian shops comes to life. See the rooms of a typical family home during the Victorian Age. Look at the military displays of memorabilia and a mock-up of a First World War trench. Marvel at the range of toys, which the more mature visitor may well remember owning.

Parks and Open Spaces

Berry Head was created at the bottom of a warm, tropical sea of the southern hemisphere some 400 million years ago. The limestone quarried here has left a noticeable hole in the side of the headland. Excellent quality limestone has been quarried here for three centuries; at its peak, some 200,000 tons a year was shipped out during the middle years of the twentieth century.

Now home to a selection of plants and animals, the English Riviera Geopark contains such diverse species as the cirl bunting, guillemot, adder, bee orchid, bloody-nose beetle, common blue butterfly, fulmar, gorse, great green bush cricket, greenfinch, porpoise, painted lady butterfly, peregrine falcon, pyramidal orchid, sloe, soay sheep, speckled wood butterfly, swallow, white rock rose and wild thyme. Staff at the park are particularly proud of the colony of greater horseshoe bats and the sightings of basking shark around the coast.

Here visitors can roam around the National Nature Reserve and the ruins of the Napoleonic fort, Second World War remains, an informative visitor centre and learning centre.

There is also the lighthouse, identified by a double white flash every fifteen seconds, which has three claims to the record books: firstly as the shortest around our coastline, at just 16ft high; secondly as the highest, as it sits atop the headland, making it soar to 207ft; and lastly, as the deepest – as it was once turned by a weight which sank slowly into a shaft plunging down 147ft, although it is now turned by an electric motor.

Brixham's Battery Grounds is now managed as an area for wild flowers – very different from its previous use as a gun battery during successive wars since the late eighteenth century. Above the marina is Bosney Gardens, a small grassy area with seating, which is a natural sun trap. At Furzeham, near the former Brixham Railway Station, is an area with a bowling green, playground and football pitch. St Mary's Park features a children's playground, tennis courts, putting green, bowling greens and large green areas.

Torquay's best known open space is Torre Abbey Meadows. Apart from the green area there is a pitch-and-putt golf course, a crazy golf attraction, crown green bowling and tennis courts. Nearby Abbey Park has a pool where ducks dabble and fountains play. At Hollicombe Park, a well-maintained area for relaxation with many shrubs and trees, a path leads underneath the railway line to Hollicombe Beach.

Corbyn Head was a gift to the council from the Mallock family in 1907. It was then heavily wooded, but the trees were decimated by Dutch elm disease. Princess Gardens on the sea front is a favourite place to relax or walk along the paths winding between the palms, flower beds, grass banks and seating. The Royal Terrace Gardens – nearly always called the Rock Walk – is planted with exotic plants and subtly illuminated after dark, providing stirring views over the bay. Directly opposite the Torquay Museum hides Torwood Gardens: a little-known area of quiet among the trees, shrubs and flowers.

At Paignton the green is used for activities throughout the tourist season, the venue for fairs, donkey rides, classic cars and BMAD (Bikers Make a Difference) bike rally during various times of the year. There is also a permanent crazy golf course and, brand new for 2012, the Geopark Playpark, representing the climate when this was washed by tropical seas. Oldway Gardens lie above the Torquay Road, a huge collection of trees and shrubs which are beautifully planted no matter the season. Crown green bowling and tennis courts are available for hire.

Palace Avenue Gardens lie towards the old town; a war memorial in this small but tastefully laid out area sits in front of the Palace Theatre. Torbay Park is almost opposite the Apollo Cinema, ornamental gardens at the front backed by a large grassy area to the rear, a safe place for children to play.

Goodrington Cliff Gardens are illuminated in the evening, tastefully designed and planted, and afford excellent views over Goodrington Sands. Below is what has become known as Youngs Park, although nobody is sure why. A boating lake, crazy golf, café and children's play area are separated from the shoreline by the promenade. Atop the Cliff Gardens is Roundham Head, a delightful area with views over the bay and a nine-hole pitch-and-putt golf course.

Babbacombe Downs are a magnet for the views these 300ft high cliffs afford over the Devon coastline to the south and, on a good day, 30 miles away along the Dorset coastline. Cary Park at St Marychurch was given by the Cary family for Queen Victoria's Diamond Jubilee in 1897. It had previously been used to stage the first Torquay horse race in 1854 but today bowling greens, tennis courts and a children's playground are the attractions.

Cayman Golf offers a unique experience in the UK. From the most dedicated golfer to those who only try their hand on the odd occasion, this is golf for everyone. Here both ball and course are designed to represent everything which can be found on a full-sized course, but for just a fraction of the cost; indeed, the cost is on a par with pitch-and-putt and crazy golf attractions nearby but much better value. The difference is in the design of the golf ball, which floats, should you encounter the water hazard, and is designed to reach a distance of approximately 70 per cent of that of a standard golf ball, making this golf for adults and children alike. Thus Cayman Golf does not mean four or five hours walking around eighteen holes; here the average is around an hour and a half. And let's face it: the enjoyment is in playing the ball, not the long walk between shots! There is also the Cayman version of a nineteenth hole, where delicious refreshments are available after the round has been played, or for those who simply wish to sit and admire the lovely view.

Businesses

Today tourism is by far the single biggest employer in the bay, meaning much of the work is seasonal (albeit with a longer season than normally found at an English resort).

Torquay Pottery is a generic term for pottery produced from the seam of terracotta clay in the grounds of the Watombe estate of the Allen family. First produced in 1869, several distinct changes were made in style and production before the last piece was made in the 1980s. Some 1,700 items are held by Torquay Museum, mostly in store, while the pieces are highly prized by collectors all over the world but particularly those from North America and Australia.

Brixham is still an important working harbour and maintains a small fishing fleet.

Suttons Seeds, a name familiar to gardeners who purchase their seeds, bulbs and related horticultural products, are based in Paignton after moving from Torquay.

Torbay People

Henry Francis Lyte (1793-1847), Scottish man of God and writer of hymns. Arriving in Brixham in April 1824, within days he set about organising education in the port. Lyte established the first Sunday school in Torbay and also a Sailors' Sunday school, with an annual treat of an outing for all. The church of St Margaret's in Brixham chimes the first few bars of *Abide With Me*, penned by Lyte when he was a resident.

Sir Humphrey Gilbert (1539-83), pioneer, adventurer, Member of Parliament and half-brother of Sir Walter Raleigh, lived at Greenway. He is particularly associated with the colonizing of Newfoundland, making numerous journeys across the Atlantic until his vessel, HMS *Squirrel*, went down with all hands on the night of 5 September 1583.

Sir Lawrence Palk (1818-83), the 4th Baronet and 1st Lord Haldon, built the Imperial Hotel and Haldon Pier in the bay, was chairman of the Torquay Hotels Co. and saw the development of the region as it took the first strides towards becoming a Mecca for tourists.

George Cary II (1769-1828) inherited Torre Abbey in the eighteenth century, the third generation of that family to hold the estate since it was purchased in 1662. The family held it until sold by Commander Henry Cary in 1930. What we see today of the abbey is largely the result of his extensive alterations carried out in the 1740s.

Roger Mallock (1772-1846), an Exeter goldsmith whose riches enabled him to purchase the manors of Cockington and Chelston in 1654. Successive generations have stamped their mark on the area: Rawlyn Mallock was among the peers who met William of Orange at Brixham in 1688 and Christopher Mallock was a good friend of Agatha Christie – she dedicated *Why Didn't they ask Evans?* to him.

Isaac Merritt (1811-74) was the eighth child of a poor family of German immigrants to Rochester, New York State. Leaving home at twelve, and with a keen and inventive mind, he eventually designed a method of improving on the current unreliable sewing machines and the Singer Company was founded. Settling in Paris to expand his business, he was forced to come to Torquay when the Franco-Prussian War broke out, staying at the Victoria and Albert Hotel before building Oldway Mansion.

Thomas Ridgeway (1543-1598) was a sixteenth-century landholder, with some 1,500 acres around St Marychurch. He purchased Torre Abbey in around 1598, a time when the place held survivors from a Spanish Armada vessel washed up in Torbay.

William Pengelly (1812-94) began his career serving on his father's ship out of Looe. Moving to Torquay in 1836, he taught at a local school before turning to lecturing and private tutoring. His scientific excavations of Kent's Cavern, following the original work by Father John MacEnery, led to him offering to prove that the Biblical chronology of Archbishop James Ussher, who had calculated the age of the Earth, was highly inaccurate.

Sue Barker (1956-) is today known as a television presenter, particularly for asking the questions on *A Question of Sport* and for the annual fortnight as the anchor for the BBC's Wimbledon coverage. Born in Paignton in April 1956, a glittering tennis career seemed to beckon after turning professional in 1973 and winning the French Open Singles title three years later, and indeed she ranked number three in the world in 1977. However, this proved to be her only victory in a major, though she reached one more singles final at the US Open in 1977. Awarded the MBE, she retired from competition in 1984.

Chris Read (1978-) was born in Paignton in August 1978, a wicketkeeper who played for Devon and Gloucestershire before joining Nottinghamshire in 1998. His fifteen tests and thirty-six One Day Internationals, spread over eight years, seem unlikely to be added to – for despite being recognised for his excellent glove work, the norm in international cricket today is for a batsman who can keep wicket rather than the reverse.

Bill Millin (1922-2010) was a Second World War Scottish piper born in Canada of Scottish parents and returned to Scotland when he was just three. Known as 'Piper Bill', he is universally remembered for playing the bagpipes during the D-Day landings in Normandy. A mainstay of Scottish and Irish soldiers for centuries, by this time the pipes were confined to the rear ranks. However, Lord Lovat ignored such orders and told Millin to play on Sword Beach during the landings. As his comrades fell about him, Billy played *Hielan' Laddie* and *The Road to the Isles*. Captured German snipers later reported that they had not targeted him, thinking him crazy. Billy Millin retired to Torquay, where he played the pipes at D-Day anniversaries until his death in 2010, aged eighty-eight.

Richard Burton (1821-90) was born in Torquay. His CV informs us he saw himself as a geographer, explorer, translator, writer, soldier, orientalist, cartographer, ethnologist, spy, linguist-poet, fencer and diplomat.

Percy Fawcett (1867-1925) was born in Torquay and a British artillery officer, archaeologist and explorer on the South American continent – where he disappeared in 1925 while looking for the ancient lost city he had named 'Z'.

Peter Cook (1937-95), a British comedian and writer born in Torquay and best remembered for his partnership with Dudley Moore.

Martin Turner (1947-), a founder member of the rock band Wishbone Ash. Born in Torquay, he was a vocalist and featured on bass guitar.

Roger Deakins (1949-), born in Torquay, is a cinematographer who had a hand in such films as *True Grit*, *A Beautiful Mind*, *The Shawshank Redemption* and *Intolerable Cruelty*.

Miranda Hart (1972-), born in Torquay. This comedienne, writer and actress made her television debut in *Hyperdrive* and earned critical acclaim for her series *Miranda*. Her father was captain of HMS *Coventry*, which hit the headlines when it was sunk during the Falklands Conflict.

Lauren Pope (1983-), born in Torquay, is a model, disk jockey, music presenter and entrepreneur who is probably best known for her role in the television series *The Only Way Is Essex*.

Lily Cole (1988-), born in Torquay, is a model and actress who made her film debut in the 2007 version of *St Trinian's*.

Torbay at War

In 1940, numerous Belgian refugees arrived in Brixham. As the number of passports could almost be counted on two hands, none were allowed past the quay until officialdom had had time to formerly identify each and every one of them, no small task.

On Roundham Head, near the cliff walk down to Goodrington, is a memorial plaque and flower bed. The details are difficult to read as the weather has taken its toll. So, before the narrative is obliterated completely, it is recorded here:

Flt. Lt Frederick Ernest Denston (1920-89)

This plaque commemorates this Memorial Garden, dedicated to PEACE and in the memory of Flt. Lt Frederick Ernest Denston, a WWII pilot who flew Spitfires throughout the war. He first saw the Torbay coastline from the air just before D-Day and vowed if he survived the war he would retire to Torbay. He realised his dream and with his wife, Peggy, walked these paths and enjoyed these gardens. After his death Peggy planned this Spitfire Garden. It was brought to fruition with the support of the Torbay Council, her present husband Wg Cdr Trevor W. Oakley AFC, the Staff and Pupils of Teign School, Kingsteignton, the Officers and Cadets of the Brixham Squadron of the Training Corps and members of the Torbay Branch of the Aircrew Association.

Blue Plaques

To date there are thirty-six plaques erected in the Torbay area to commemorate local people or events. So diverse are the reasons behind their erection that the only real link between them is their location. This list is given in the best chronological order of the events and people commemorated.

Torquay – **Torre Abbey**, The King's Drive. Built around the end of the twelfth century, what is now known as the Spanish Barn held 397 Spanish prisoners in July 1688, remnants of the failed Armada.

Torquay – Fleet Street, the **First Torquay Methodist Church** was opened in 1807, twenty years after John Wesley and his brother Charles first came to this part of the country on their preaching tours.

Torquay – **Madreport Place** was the site of the town's first educational establishment in 1826, when building of the Torquay National School began.

Torquay – Beacon Hill saw poet **Elizabeth Barrett Browning** in residence for three years from 1838.

Torquay – **The Palace Hotel**, Babbacombe Road, was built in 1841 as Bishopstowe, the home of Henry Phillpotts, Bishop of Exeter (1831–60). George Sands opened this as a hotel in 1921.

Torquay – Woodfield, Lower Woodfield Road was home to **Edward Vivian MA JP** from 1842. During his fifty-one years here he was renowned as both a banker and for his tireless work for the poor.

Torquay – Lower Warberry Road where **Normount**, now the Bishops Court Hotel, was built in 1844 by the Harvey Brothers, renowned local architects and developers.

Torquay – **Erith House**, Lower Erith Road, was established in 1860 and named after Lady Eardley of Erith, Kent. It replaced Torquay Institution, here from 1845, a home for 'gentlewomen of limited means' who came to Torbay to benefit from the mild climate, thought to alleviate health problems.

Torquay – near the eastern end of Lower Warberry Road is **Vomero**, the first home of **Isambard Kingdom Brunel** in the area. His stay here was brief: July to November 1848, while he and his wife finalised arrangements for his estate further north along the coastline at Watcombe.

Torquay – **Barn Close**, Watcombe Beach Road, was a planned estate of homes for the workers of Isambard Kingdom Brunel from the late 1840s on.

Paignton – The Redcliffe was designed by **Colonel Robert Smith** (1787–1873), an engineer, artist and architect who made his name in India before making this his home in 1852.

Paignton – **Bishops Place** saw four homes built in 1857 by Isambard Kingdom Brunel for the doctor, architect, engineer and supplies manager of the South Devon Railway.

PAIGNTON PRESERVATION & LOCAL HISTORY SOCIETY • TORBAY CIVIC SOCIETY

FORTIFICATIONS OF
**THE PALACE OF THE
BISHOPS OF EXETER**

**LORDS OF THE MANOR
OF PEINTONA
1050 - 1549**

THE ORIGINAL BLUE PLAQUE
WAS ERECTED HERE IN 1987.
THIS PLAQUE WAS UNVEILED FOLLOWING
THE REFURBISHMENT OF THE
BISHOPS TOWER, COURTESY OF
THE HERITAGE LOTTERY FUND,
AND THE RE-OPENING OF
THE TOWER IN 2007.

2007

Torquay – Meadfoot House, Hesketh Crescent earns its blue plaque for a visit of just six short weeks in the summer of 1861. However, the stature of this man certainly merits the plaque, for this was where naturalist, traveller, geologist and author of *On the Origin of Species* **Charles Robert Darwin** (1809–82) stayed.

Torquay – Montpelier Road. The **Church of St John the Evangelist** is a Grade I listed building begun in 1861 and completed in 1885 from a design by G.E. Street.

Paignton – Broadsands Road's most imposing construction is the **Hookhills Viaduct**. Taking four years to complete, **Isambard Kingdom Brunel**'s railway crossed the 85ft high, 116-yard long viaduct's nine arches for the first time in 1864.

Paignton – **Oldway Mansion** was completed in 1874 by **Isaac Merritt Singer**. The present building is the result of adaptations by his son, Paris Singer. The family name has been found on sewing machines for more than a century, and his modifications brought the technology into the homes of millions.

Torquay – The Terrace was home to artist **John Salter** (1825–91), who lived and worked here for twelve years from 1878. His daughter Mary donated some forty of his works to Torquay Museum.

Paignton – The **Paignton Club** was founded in 1882, in a Grade II building which stands at the southern end of Paignton promenade, and offers private membership to residents of the borough.

Brixham – the theatre in New Road opened its doors for the first time in 1887; built at a cost of £3,000, it originally seated 800.

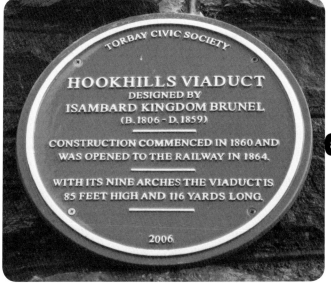

TORBAY CIVIC SOCIETY

HOOKHILLS VIADUCT
DESIGNED BY
ISAMBARD KINGDOM BRUNEL
(B. 1806 - D. 1859)

CONSTRUCTION COMMENCED IN 1860 AND
WAS OPENED TO THE RAILWAY IN 1864.

WITH ITS NINE ARCHES THE VIADUCT IS
85 FEET HIGH AND 116 YARDS LONG.

2006

Torquay – Eltham, Oak Hill Road, Ashfield, was home to **Eden Phillpotts** for twenty-eight years, from 1888 onwards. Author of more than 300 books during the ninety-eight years of his life, he is best remembered for the eighteen novels known as the Dartmoor Cycle, still popular even though many editions are out of print.

Paignton – currently Barclays Bank, Palace Avenue was home to **Oliver Heaviside** from 1889 until 1897. A Fellow of the Royal Society and a renowned mathematician and scientist, his electromagnetic theories and predictions resulted in the Heaviside Layer being named after him. This atmospheric layer was being used to bounce radio waves in the longer band widths around the curvature of the Earth prior to the use of artificial satellites in orbit.

Torquay – Oak Hill Road, Ashfield, was the birthplace and early home of Agatha Miller from 1890. By the time of her death in 1976 she was world famous as author **Dame Agatha Christie**, forever known as the Queen of Crime.

Babbacombe – Beach Road, aptly very close to Babbacombe Theatre, was the home of one of our nation's most famous playwrights during the winter of 1892-3, **Oscar Wilde**.

Torquay – Rock House, Rock House Lane, was home to the celebrated author **Rudyard Kipling** for two years following his return from America in 1896.

Torquay – Orestone, Rock House Lane, was a holiday home of **John Calcott Horsley**, close friend and relative of Isambard Kingdom Brunel until his death in 1903, aged eighty-six. An artist, he is best known as the designer of the first Christmas card.

Torquay – **Torquay Boys' Grammar School**, Rock Road, opened as the Torquay Pupil Teachers Centre on 4 September 1904.

Torquay – Riviera Court (then Cleave Court), Stitchill Road, was home to author, playwright, journalist, composer and public speaker **Beverley Nichols** (1898-1983) for eleven years from 1913.

Brixham – Berry Head Road, just west of the junction with Victoria Road, was the boyhood home of **Leonard James Callaghan** (1914-2005). He was an MP (1945-87) and leader of the Labour Party (1976-80) – during which time he served as Prime Minister – and Lord Callaghan of Cardiff from 1987 until his death in 2005. 'Sunny' Jim Callaghan frequently returned to the home he knew until he was ten years old; he had been a pupil at Furzeham Primary School.

Torquay – At **Overgang** is a plaque dedicated to the 'Heroes of the *Provident*, BM 291'. Built in 1910, this fishing smack was lost on 28 November 1916 when attacked by the German submarine UB-37 off Portland Bill. There were no casualties.

Paignton – **Primley House**, Totnes Road, was home to the Belfield family before Herbert Whitley moved here and opened his private collection of animals to the public in 1923. Later the Primley Zoological Gardens became Paignton Zoo.

Cockington – **Cockington Court** had been the manor house for the Squires of Cockington for longer than records exist, but certainly since the Saxon era. The date on the plaque of 1932 is chosen simply as it was then that the property ceased to be privately owned.

Cockington – the Drum Inn opened its doors in 1936, the work of the famous architect **Sir Edwin Landseer Lutyens** OM KCIE PRA FRIBA, chosen for his reputation for adapting older architectural styles into a later era and thus maintaining the character of the village.

Brixham – New Road became home to novelist **Flora Thompson** in 1940, living here until her death in 1947 aged seventy. The last book in the trilogy of *Lark Rise to Candleford* – the whole of which has been recently televised – was written during Flora Thompson's stay in Brixham.

Brixham – Vale House, Manor Vale Road, Galmpton, was home to novelist and poet **Robert Graves** for six years from 1940. The building itself is a former farmhouse dating from the seventeenth century.

Babbacombe – 22 Princes Street was home to **Clifford R. Cooksley** on 30 May 1943. He was killed within sight of his home during a bombing raid. At just sixteen years of age, he was the youngest Civil Defence Messenger casualty in the region.

Brixham – 73 South Furzeham Road became home to **John Chancellor** in 1963. The previous thirty years of his life spent at sea, he settled in Brixham – where he developed a reputation as one of the great modern maritime artists until his death in 1984.

Folklore

Daddyhole Plain takes its name from Daddy Hole, the chasm in the cliff face where the Devil is said to reside. Indeed this is the origin of the name, a corruption of 'Deddy', a local name for Satan.

According to the legend, a strange thing happened to a young girl who was wandering here one evening, reflecting on her unrequited love for a young man. Suddenly, she became aware of the baying of hounds and the thunder of hooves. Turning, she beheld a fearful sight: the Devil himself astride an enormous horse. She fainted. Waking, she found a young man bending over her. While recovering from her ordeal they conversed and she learned that he, too, suffered from unrequited love. There and then they made a pact: together they would exact vengeance upon the source of their troubles.

Several meetings ensued until one day he came to her with news that the source of her affections and the girl he had his heart set on had become lovers and that they would be meeting the next evening on Daddyhole Plain. She arrived to find the man she desired and his mistress in each other's arms. Before they realised what was happening both were stabbed, wounds which were deep and mortal.

As their lives ebbed away, a great storm blew up – and the phantom hunt bore down on the woman a second time. She turned her head just in time to see her partner in crime urging on the lead horse. He bent to lift her to his saddle – and then all three leaped over the cliff and into Daddy's Hole.

The murderess was never seen again.

Oak Apple Day is 29 May, chosen to represent the official date of the Restoration, the birthday of Charles II. In later centuries boys and girls of Devon would wear garlands of gilded oak apples and leaves, dancing through the streets in celebration. Each carried a bunch of freshly picked nettles with which they would thrash those children who were not wearing oak leaves to celebrate the Restoration.

William of Orange landed at Brixham on 5 November 1688. This was re-enacted by his descendant exactly 300 years later, Queen Elizabeth II unveiling the statue which now stands on the harbourside. However, the two events were a little different, for Prince William arrived at low tide.

A local man named Varwell saw his predicament and walked out to carry the future king on his back to the safety of the shore. William was delighted to hear the church bells ringing out to announce his arrival; nobody could bring themselves to tell him they had been rung every year on this day since 1606, the first anniversary of the Gunpowder Plot. Meanwhile, Varwell continued to push himself forward and led the London-bound procession as far as Newton Abbot. Here, the delighted king gave Varwell a document enabling him to come to London to claim his reward following the coronation.

Returning to Brixham to gather a few belongings for the journey, he boasted of his reward in every inn and tavern he frequented from South Devon to the capital. During one particularly heavy drinking session with new-found friends in London – who kept him in an inebriated state for more than a week – his document was stolen. One of their number went to the palace to claim the reward, which amounted to £100, in his place. When sober, Varwell also went to visit the king to claim his reward but was denounced as an impostor and returned home to Devon empty-handed.

Interestingly, friends and relatives later maintained that his time in the capital was a story concocted by Varwell so he would not have to share a single penny of his windfall.

Pier Inn overlooks Paignton Harbour and has done for as long as this has been a resort. A series of unexplained people and events have been reported over the years. A little girl appears in a bedroom in the living quarters. No longer does she frighten: indeed, those who meet her consider her part of the charm of the place. A neighbour living behind the property often sees a number of individuals gathered around a table near an open fire in the early hours.

Earlier the place was known as the Harbour Bar and was much smaller, with fisherman's cottages sitting either side. A ghostly old fisherman has been seen sitting on the steps by a local hotelier who called in for a drink. Another fisherman, this time accompanied by a woman, has often been witnessed turning to pass through a rear wall. Perhaps these are memories of that earlier time?

Isambard Kingdom Brunel spent much of the last ten years of his life in Torbay, renting a villa at St Marychurch. Both he and Mary, his wife, were involved in many local projects, she opening the school at Barton.

Almost immediately after his death, the Little Giant, as he was known, was seen wearing his trademark stovepipe hat around the streets of St Marychurch and Babbacombe. One drunk watched as he walked up to and through the locked doors of the church, whereupon the most eerie music was heard from within. Such an experience instantly sobered the witness: he ran home as fast as he could, never to touch another drop for the rest of his days.

Churston Court Inn is a twelfth-century coaching inn. Adjacent to the old church and its farm, it retains many original features including four-poster beds, stone windows, original staircases, oak panelling and flagstone floors, giving it a Grade I Listing. An old monk is said to appear in that part of the building formerly used as the kitchens. Hooded and gowned, the ghost appears and melts away into the ancient stone walls.

Sailing and Smuggling

Brixham's harbour has been the principal home of fishing in the bay since the early sixteenth century. Paignton's harbour, also once used by fishermen, is today used solely by pleasure craft. Torquay's harbour was once primarily used by fishermen bringing home thier catch, although since the growth of the resort its harbour has become the home to the marina with its impressive array of privately owned vessels. Few realise that there was once a fourth harbour in the bay (a map from the sixteenth century shows a harbour at Livermead).

Brixham was the birthplace of the sailing trawler, a traditional fishing boat which formed the fleet in Brixham from the nineteenth century. Elegant vessels, they inspired artists and even songwriters – 'Red Sails in the Sunset' was written in 1935 by Hugh Williams about the trawler *Torbay Lass*. At their peak there were some 300 vessels in Brixham alone, nearly all in private ownership (and usually the property of the skipper). They were in regular use right up to the Second World War.

The first lifeboat in the bay appeared in 1866. A sudden wind change on the night of 10-11 January brought a hurricane from the southeast. The strong winds accompanied by heavy sleet forced sixty or seventy ships to shelter in the bay. Yet forty of those vessels were destroyed, with the loss of around 100 lives. A second lifeboat was stationed at Torquay ten years later, only to close in 1923 when the first motorised lifeboat was stationed at Brixham and renamed *Torbay* the following year.

Upham's Shipyard in Brixham constructed a replica of the seventeenth-century ship *Mayflower* in 1955-6. A collaboration between the Plimouth Plantation, an American museum and journalist Warwick Charlton, and financed by private donation, *Mayflower II* was to recreate the journey of the original, taking the Pilgrims to the New World. It sailed westwards on its one and only voyage in 2002, under the command of Alan Villiers, and is now a permanent floating museum near Plymouth Rock, Massachusetts, where its namesake traditionally landed.

As a crime, smuggling was effectively created by the Smugglers Act, which was passed to curb the problem of tax avoidance on such things as brandy, tea and tobacco. Local fishermen supplemented their meagre income by bringing brandy back from Roskoff and St Malo. From Durl Head through to Man Sands, the coastline saw a constant stream of craft visiting drop-off points.

Near the shore, kegs would be dropped to the sea bed, weighted by stones and attached to long ropes allowing floats to mark their position. Whenever possible, kegs were floated in on the incoming tide, enabling them to be dropped much further out to sea. In order to hide the cargo from searching excise men while at sea, kegs were tethered to the keel.

When the cargo reached the shore, under cover of darkness, runners would take it to their inland destination: taverns, which they knew as kiddly-winks. Runners had two ponies; each carried two kegs of brandy, with the runner riding them alternately. Villagers and townsfolk would turn a blind eye to smuggling activities, yet to guarantee they were left alone, many took to wearing a white sheet to scare away superstitious inhabitants when passing through residential areas.

Bob Elliott of Brixham was a particularly successful smuggler. So much contraband was passing through his hands that his distribution network could not take everything being landed and soon all his coastal hiding places – caves, stashes buried in the sand, etc – were full.

So when another load arrived he was forced to bring it to his cottage, just what the watching excise men were waiting for. On the day they came knocking, Elliott was laid up with gout. However, when the door opened his grieving family informed the excise men that he had died the previous night, which put off any search.

Later that day a large coffin for a large man arrived to carry the body away. On the road the party were confronted by the excise officers but fled when they saw the ghost of the deceased bringing up the rear. When their superior heard the terrifying tale, he grew suspicious and headed straight round to the Elliott household. Eavesdropping outside, he heard Bob boasting of how he had fooled his staff, whereupon he burst in upon the now ashen-faced smugglers.

However, Bob Elliott had the last laugh, for, without proof, no prosecution resulted.

Shipwrecks

Known for its mild, sub-tropical climate, freak weather systems along the coastline here come from just one direction – the open ocean to the east. Although seen as a safe haven, over the last 250 years the bay has averaged almost one wreck a year.

Not that these are evenly spread over this period, for on 28 November 1916 a German submarine was responsible for sinking four vessels in a single day – *Catena*, *Diligence*, *Sea Lar* and *Vulcan* – off Berry Head. These were all privately owned vessels out of Brixham and sunk using only a machine gun.

When *Tiger* was wrecked off Berry Head by a hurricane on 27 February 1745, 170 soldiers were drowned when *en route* to the West Indies to relieve existing forces. While February 1762 saw the sinking of the vessel which gave its name to Savage Hole, that part of the coast against which it was wrecked.

However by far the heaviest toll occurred on 10 January 1866 when a hurricane hit the bay leaving a trail of destruction which included the loss of: *Abeona*, *Alona*, *Amanda*, *Belle*, *Britannia*, *Briton*, *Ceasarwitch*, *Cambria*, *Courier*, *Dryan*, *Elizabeth Lewis*, *Ellen Edwards*, *Emille & Charles*, *Ernest*, *Florence Nightingale*, *Forerunner*, *Grace*, *Hanover*, *Helen*, *Honor*, *Jacoba*, *James*, *Jessy*, *Lady of the Lake*, *Leone*, *Liveley*, *Margaret Ann*, *Monda*, *Providence*, *Salem*, *Scythian*, *Sky*, *Telegraph*, and *Wild Rose*.

Species and Recipes

The region is synonymous with the so-called Torbay Palm, the image adopted by the English Riviera Tourist Board as it represents the renowned mild climate. However, the species is neither native to Torbay, nor is it a palm tree. Found growing elsewhere in the country, this is *Cordyline Australis*, native to New Zealand and also known as the cabbage tree.

A cabbage which does have much closer ties to the region was grown in fields reclaimed from the sea and occupying the area in front of the Palace Theatre and around Palace Avenue. From the early nineteenth century the famous Paignton Flat Poll cabbage was grown here, leading to Paignton people being known as Flat-Polls.

Earlier Paignton residents were referred to as 'Pudden-eaters'. The Paignton pudding has been a part of the town's history since the thirteenth century. On the granting of the town charter, part payment to the Crown came in the form of a pudding recorded as both 'white-pot' and 'bag pudding'. Various references are made to the pudding over the centuries, although whether it was ever truly made annually is a mystery.

The first recipe appears in 1819, stated as being 'an ancient custom revived for the fair'. A local bakery provided '400lbs of flour, 170lbs of suet, 140lbs of raisins, and 20 dozen eggs' to be boiled in the brewing copper of the Crown & Anchor. Not that this huge creation was to be sent to the king: after four days of cooking it was taken to the Green (on a waggon drawn by eight oxen) and distributed to the poor. Since then the pudding has been reserved for special events, such as the coming of the railways in 1859, a charity fund-raiser in 1895, the carnival of 1930 and to raise money for Paignton Hospital League of Friends in 1968.

Sport

Brixham Rugby Football Club, who play their home matches at Astley Park, are nicknamed the Fishermen. The earliest record of Rugby Union dates from 1850, when a newly ordained curate arrived from Cambridge University and arranged a rough form of the game for local fishermen. In existence from 1874, the club is one of only six surviving founder members of Devon RFU. Initially games were played on Furzeham Green, until moving to the present ground in 1896. Rescued from financial troubles by two local men, Astley and Smardon, they returned ownership to the club on the understanding no rates would be levied on the ground. That exemption is still in operation.

In this Olympic Year of 2012, it is fitting to look back at a previous time. In 1948, the yachting events were held in Torbay. Five classes of boat were competed in by twenty-five countries over seven days, seventy-five vessels in all. Because of the quality of the racing, nothing was decided until the final day – and, even then, some medals were unknown until the very last minute of the last race, which was considered the greatest competition in the 175-year history of the sport.

Gold medals were presented on that last day to the USA, Norway, Denmark and Great Britain and, following the playing of these anthems, the camaraderie of the competitors was seen as everyone linked hands in a spontaneous rendering of *Auld Lang Syne*. One competitor summed up this week: 'I have been a-yachting, man and boy, these forty years. Now, having seen Torbay 1948, I could cheerfully prepare to chant my *Nunc dimittis*, not presuming to hope to see again an occasion to match it in completeness and perfection.'

Paignton Rugby Club was founded in 1873, moving to its present home of Queens Park in 1902. It is a former salt marsh which was filled in, by locals, one cartload at a time. Rugby League has been played here since the 1980s. The ground doubles as the cricket club during the summer months. Currently three teams appear in the Devon Cricket League, with a fourth hoping to join them soon. Added to this are teams representing Sunday, Midweek, T20 and Colts sides (of all age groups).

Torquay Football Club, known as the Gulls, is a result of the merger of three clubs: Torquay Town, Ellacombe and Babbacombe. Originally the club played in a dark blue and light blue strip. By the time they played their first league match, in August 1927, this had changed to black and white; the current blue and gold strip was adopted in 1954. Torquay's first ever promotion was in season 1960; they appeared at Wembley in 1984. Among the more famous names associated with the club are Frank O'Farrell, Bruce Rioch, Roy McFarland, Cyril Knowles and David Webb as managers; former internationals John Bond, Ken Brown, Eddie Kelly and Tony Currie appeared for the club, while their most famous exports were Colin Lee, who signed for Tottenham Hotspur for £60,000 in October 1977, and seventeen-year-old Lee Sharpe, who left for Manchester United in a deal worth £180,000 in 1988.

Coastal Path

Of all the walks around the bay, the longest and most spectacular is undoubtedly the South West Coast Path. From Brixham to Babbacombe is 13 miles of undulating coastline ranging from sea level to 909ft above high tide. Among the many highlights are Brixham Battery, Fishcombe Cove, Elberry Cove, Broadsands Beach, Saltern Cove, Oyster Cove, Goodrington Beach, Roundham Head, Fairy Cove, Paignton Harbour, Paignton Sands, Paignton Pier, Preston Sands, Hollicombe Beach, Livermead, Torre Abbey, Torquay Harbour, Daddyhole Plain, Meadfoot Beach, Anstey's Cove, Babbacombe Beach, Cliff Railway and Oddicombe Beach.

Aside from the sand and pebbles of the beaches, it affords views of the Paignton and Dartmouth Steam Railway (from above as well as below), the chance for a huge range of refreshment possibilities at Paignton, Torquay and Babbacombe, and numerous other distractions – including several ways to play golf!

Local Dialect

Aimzes – pronounced 'hames' – reins.

Ay–jey–boar – hedgehog.

Bellerziz – bellows.

Brown titus – bronchitis.

Cracked – correct.

Crap o' teddies – crop of potatoes.

Drish – thrush (the bird).

Drot – throat.

Dummun – old woman.

Eel – hill.

Erbons – ribbons.

Fey – faith.

Furnt – front.

Ginst – towards.

Grockle – holidaymaker, visitor.

Gwaine – going.

Hengous – terrible.

Holly – shout.

Iss – yes.

Izzel – himself.

Jean – gin.

Jumbo-zale – jumble sale.

Kit – bird of prey.

Leel – little.

Louster – littering.

Margit – market.

Mazed – daft.

Mokus – monkey.

Nair – mean, tight-fisted.

Nointed – wicked.

On-wriggler – uneven.

Ormers – alms.

Owzum–iver – however.

Pankin – panting.

Pawer – to cram full.

Pisky laid – caused to be lost (by the pixies).

Pool – top of the head.

Quelstring – hot (weather).

Rames – skeleton.

Rile – royal.

Scabby – a dirty trick.

Sex – sect of a church.

Shape – sheep.

Shitten – contemptible.

Spuddlin – poking about.

Steve – to freeze.

Toze – to comb.

Twadden – a denial.

Upzot – upset.

Vahl – a fall of snow.

Vall – autumn.

Vittles – food.

Vurriner – someone from the next village.

Wopsey – wasp.

Wuts – oats.

Yawcat – female cat.

Yurrin – a trial.

Zad – the last letter of the alphabet.

Zin – sun.

Zoonder – rather.

Tried and Tested

One of Torquay's hidden treasures is Camelot, a pub restaurant providing an extensive menu. A real taste of home.

The most excellent cream tea, with home-baked scones, can be found at the tea rooms in Cockington Manor.

For an evening meal or lunchtime treat, the Cary Arms at Babbacombe and the Redcliffe Hotel at Paignton take a lot of beating. Worthwhile booking in advance.

The Pier Inn near Paignton Harbour offers a free quiz on Sunday evenings with prizes for all competitors and the chance of a desirable cash prize for the winners. Every week there is a free pool night, and during the season you can find entertainment every night, with bands also appearing out of season. Three rooms plus a rooftop garden offer something for everyone.

A warm welcome, comfortable rooms, the best of breakfasts and unbeatable value for money await at the Three Palms Hotel in Sands Road. David and Veronica also have a well-stocked bar.

Brixham Fish and Chips on The Quay, Brixham, offer a sumptuous and well-presented meal which cannot be beaten for the price.

Squires, on the corner of Dartmouth Road and Broadsands Road and opposite Churston Library, is as far from a chip shop as a fish restaurant could be.

Embassy Tavern has a jam night on Wednesdays, but please don't bring auntie's preserve – although you are welcome to bring a guitar, keyboard, harmonica or just your voice. This is the absolute best of local musicians and singers who put together an excellent and impromptu set, which is never the same twice.

George Goodridge

Born 22 May 1796, Charles Medyett Goodridge was incorrectly recorded as George in the writings of Sabine Baring-Gould – and the name has stuck. This is but a small example of the ill-fortune which was to plague this man's life. His maritime career began at thirteen, as a cabin boy aboard the *Lord Cochrane*; he then joined the crew of the *Prince of Wales*, bound for the South Seas, in May of the following year.

This vessel was on a voyage of sealing and trading. By November 1820 they had arrived at the Crozet Islands where frequent storms and snow, a complete lack of vegetation, and an extraordinary run of bad luck left the crew divided between two islands, with each believing the other lost and drowned. In December the following year the captain, his brother, young Goodridge and five others made the crossing in a small boat they had been using for shelter in an attempt to find a way home.

Reunited, the fifteen-man crew used what little they had to create shelter from the stones which had once provided the ballast for the ship and its wooden planks. With ingenuity Crusoe would have been proud of, the men set to the task of building a vessel to get them off the island. After almost two years' work – and with their vessel almost ready for departure – a massive storm wrecked it.

Their luck changed in January 1823 when a passing vessel was spotted and attracted by a signal fire. Taken to what is now Tasmania, they landed at Hobart on 7 July – where Goodridge was promptly arrested. Suspected of being a deserter and thrown into prison, bush rangers meted out their own brand of justice with routine beatings to within an inch of his life.

Eventually he arrived back in Torbay in 1831, shortly after the death of his father, taking a wife the following year. For some inexplicable reason he had a desire to return to Tasmania, but his aging mother kept him at home. In 1837 he wrote of his travels (with a typically snappy book title of the day) in *A Narrative of a Voyage to the South Seas and a Shipwreck of the Prince of Wales*. This ran to six editions, and in the fourth he spoke of his further misfortunes since his return to England: a failed inn at Dartmouth and a shop at Brixham, adding his only means of support were the monies he received from the book.

At the time he was just forty-five years of age.

Dame Agatha Christie

Known as a best-selling authoress (as she called herself), Dame Agatha's infamous missing eleven days are almost as well-known as her fiction. Also well known is the continuous performance of *The Mousetrap* since its opening night on 25 November 1952. She has sold some four billion copies of her books worldwide, translated into more than 100 languages. When added to those from films and stage performances, they still realise annual royalty payments of more than £3 million.

Less well known are the many criminals who have copied the scenarios in her books. While it could be argued the perpetrators were unaware they were acting out the work of fiction, this was not so in two examples. What was then West Germany in 1981 saw a murder mirroring that seen in *Murder on the Orient Express*, while two years earlier, in the US state of North Carolina, a copycat murder was uncovered, one investigated by Jane Marple in *Sleeping Murder*.

In 1974 Albert Finney portrayed Hercule Poirot in the film *Murder on the Orient Express*. This generated renewed interest in the book and saw sales of three million in the year of release, exactly forty years after it was first published. Dame Agatha often spoke of her favourite author, Charles Dickens. One of her novels, written under the pseudonym Mary Westmacott, was published in 1944. Entitled *Absent in the Spring*, it took Christie just three days to write.

Captions and Credits

Page:

3. Coat of arms, granted in May 1968

7. Churston Manor and its church

9. Paignton Pier; the road named after the man who built the pier

11. Memorial Clock Tower, Torquay

13. Entrance to the Napoleonic Fort, Berry Head

15. Beach huts at Broadsands

17. Torquay Harbour from the top of the rocky outcrop which gave the place its name

19. The Torquay land train

21. Fisher Street; the Pavilions, Torquay; Knick Knack Lane

23. Redcliffe Hotel, Paignton; Gerston Place; Goodrington Cliff Walk

25 Signpost on Berry Head

27. Hamelin Way

28 William Pengelly (courtesy of Torquay Museum); statue of William of Orange

29. St Matthew's church, Chelston; Coverdale Tower, Paignton

30. Tower Road, named after Coverdale Tower

31. Coverdale Road, also named after Coverdale Tower

32. Look up so as not to miss the architecture in Torwood Street, Torquay

33. Quaywest water park, Goodrington

37. No humble sea food stall, Claws has been copied as a model for the popular *Lilliput Lane* series; the Palace Theatre, Paignton

39. Berry Head's lighthouse

41. Briefcase (Jean Scheijen)

43. Paignton Harbour at low tide; Quay West from the very top of the slides (courtesy of Quay West); the marina at Torquay

45. The infamous balloon officially known as the Torquay Hi Flyer

47. The Gleneagles Hotel

49. Overlooking the beach at Goodrington

51. Churston's church

53. Kirkham House, Paignton

55. A novel advertisement for the brand new state-of-the-art library at Paignton

57. *The Golden Hind*

59. Paignton parish church at the end of Winner Street; the Seashore Centre, Goodrington

61. The tip of Berry Head from sea level. Quarrying is again evident, (courtesy of Benjamin S. Schwarz)

62 Common dolphins off Berry Head (courtesy of Mark Darlaston); views from Berry Head; leaping common dolphins off Berry Head (courtesy of Mark Darlaston)

63. Remains of the Napoleonic defences on Berry Head; bottle nose dolphins off Berry Head (courtesy of Mark Darlaston)

65. Pitch and putt at Torquay

67. Torwood Gardens; duck pond near Torquay Station; Torre Abbey

69. Waterbirds are common on the lake at Youngs Park, Goodington; nobody has any idea why this solitary grave, the last resting place of Major Thomas Hill, should be situated in the very centre of Youngs Park, Goodrington

71. A green at Cayman Golf (courtesy of Su Limmer, manager of Cayman Golf); less yardage but at least the equal in beauty (courtesy of Su Limmer, manager of Cayman Golf); Caymon Golf's version of the nineteenth hole (courtesy of Su Limmer, manager of Cayman Golf)

73. An impressive mural tucked away at the side of a building in Gerston Place, Paignton; Torquay Museum; Camelot, Torquay (courtesy of Benjamin S. Schwarz); The Manor Inn, Churston Ferrers

75. Palk Street, Torquay

77. St Matthew's church, Chelston

79. Spanish Armada

83. Memorial to Lieutenant Commander Arthur Leyland Harrison VC RN, a Torquay man killed in action on St George's Day, 1918; war memorial at Torquay

85. Torre Abbey, which held prisoners from the Spanish Armada

87. Blue plaque on the Bishop's Tower, Paignton

89. Blue plaque on the Hookhills Viaduct, Broadsands Road

91. Plaque in memory of Oliver Heaviside; the boat that takes tourists along the Dart to visit Agatha Christie's home at Greenway; the old bus that takes visitors to Greenway House

93. Herbert Whitley, founder of Paignton Zoo (courtesy of Paignton Zoo)

95. Hollicombe Beach

97. Daddyhole near Torquay (courtesy of Benjamin S. Schwarz)

99. William of Orange (courtesy of the Library of Congress, LC-USZ62-54812)

101. An unusual commemorative display of the Golden Jubilee of Queen Elizabeth II in 2002; the parish church of St Mary, St Marychurch; church of St Mary the Virgin, Churston; the Pier Inn, Paignton

103. Trawlers leaving harbour (courtesy of the Library of Congress, LC-DIG-ppmsc-08055)

105. *Mayflower II* (photograph courtesy of Plimoth Plantation, USA)

107. Brixham from the harbour (courtesy of the Library of Congress, LC-DIG-ppmsc-08054)

109. Waves crashing on Institute Beach

111. The Torbay palm; natural flora atop Berry Head (courtesy of Benjamin S. Schwarz)

113. Brixham rugby in action (courtesy of Philip Wills); Brixham start their rugby players young (courtesy of Philip Wills)

115. Torquay's players, directors, staff and supporters (courtesy of Tim Herbert, Torquay United Football Club)

117. Steam train pulled by Goliath coming up the incline over Goodrington Sands on its way to Kingswear (courtesy of Jonathan Poulton-Smith); the coastal path may have taken a different route had quarrying not removed this part of Berry Head; the promenade along Preston Sands

121. An idyllic rural summer scene as the village cricket team take to the field with Cockington Manor in the background (courtesy of Benjamin S. Schwarz); The Cary Arms, Babbacombe (courtesy of Benjamin S. Shwarz)

124. Books (SXC)

Bibliography

Shipwreck Index of the British Isles by Richard and Bridget Larn
The Book of Brixham: Portrait of a Harbour Town by Frank Pearce
The Folklore of Devon by Ralph Whitlock
Devon Ghosts and Legends by Mike Holgate
A Dictionary of Devon Dialect by John Downes
A Torbay Century by John Pike and the *Herald Express*